ABSTRACTS FROM

History of Cherry Valley
[New York]
from 1740 to 1898
BY
John Sawyer

— AND —

The Story of the Massacre at Cherry Valley
A PAPER READ BY
Mrs. William S. Little

DECEMBER 12TH, 1890

BEFORE THE
ROCHESTER HISTORICAL SOCIETY
AND PUBLISHED
AT THE REQUEST OF THE SOCIETY

HERITAGE BOOKS
2011

HERITAGE BOOKS
AN IMPRINT OF HERITAGE BOOKS, INC.

Books, CDs, and more—Worldwide

For our listing of thousands of titles see our website
at
www.HeritageBooks.com

A Facsimile Reprint
Published 2011 by
HERITAGE BOOKS, INC.
Publishing Division
100 Railroad Ave. #104
Westminster, Maryland 21157

Published in 1993
by Pipe Creek Publications

— Publisher's Notice —
In reprints such as this, it is often not possible to remove blemishes from the original. We feel the contents of this book warrant its reissue despite these blemishes and hope you will agree and read it with pleasure.

International Standard Book Numbers
Paperbound: 978-1-58549-669-3
Clothbound: 978-0-7884-8802-3

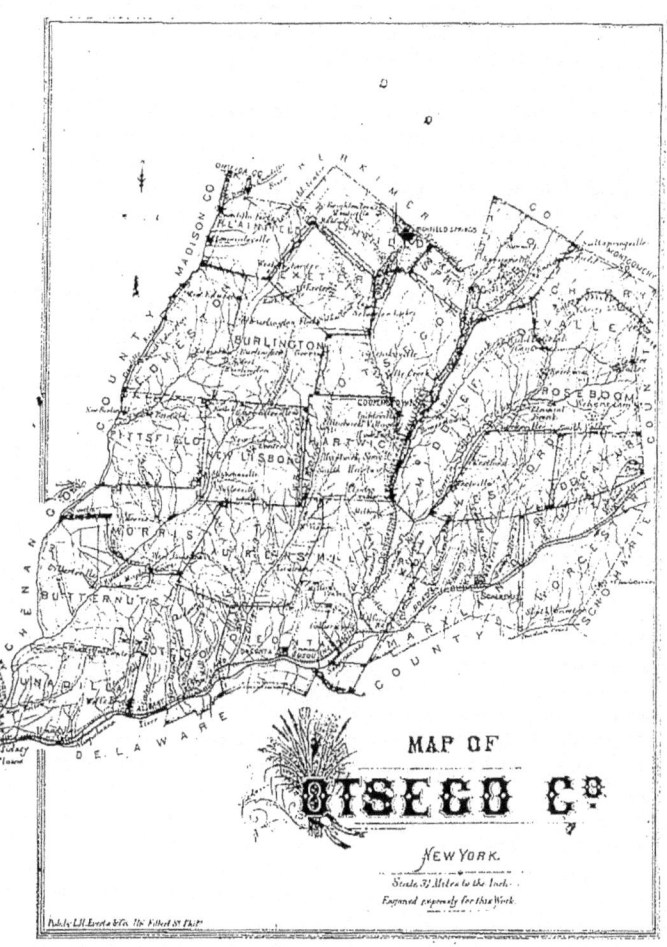

The writer wishes to acknowledge her indebtedness to the kind criticism and suggestions of her relatives and friends, as well as to the following sources of information:

1. "Annals of Tyron County, or the Border Warfare of New York during the Revolution," by William W. Campbell, LL.D.

2. "Central New York in the Revolution," Address delivered by Douglas Campbell, Esq., at the unveiling of a monument in commemoration of the massacre at Cherry Valley.

3. "An Historical Account of the Presbyterian Church at Cherry Valley, N. Y.," by Rev. H. U. Swinnerton, Ph. D.

4. The Journal of Wm. McKendry, a lieutenant in the army of the Revolution, and an original member of the Society of the Cincinnati, published by the Massachusetts Historical Society, and furnished by the courtesy of Mr. Andrew McFarland Davis of the American Antiquarian Society.

5. A Book of "Memorabilia," relating to Cherry Valley, collected by Mr. Rufus A. Grider, of Canajoharie, N. Y.

THE MASSACRE AT CHERRY VALLEY.

"There are fatal days indeed
In which the fibrous years have taken root
So deeply, that they quiver to their tops,
Whene'er you stir the dust of such a day."

The question is often asked: "Where is Cherry Valley, and why is it so well known?"

First, let us look at its location, for this goes far to explain its prominence. It is situated fifty miles southwest of Albany, as the crow flies, just over the crest and on the southern side of the watershed between the Mohawk and Susquehanna rivers. Cold spring, a mile from the village limits, is the head waters of one of the tributaries of the Mohawk river, which is twelve miles to the north, and in the spring of the year its waters almost mingle with those of one of the longest branches of the Susquehanna river, the Cherry Valley creek, flowing in a southerly direction.

Six miles away, to the west, over a steep hill, lies Otsego lake, whose beautiful waters and wooded shores have been immortalized by Fenimore Cooper's pen. The village, now containing only a thousand inhabitants, lies nearly midway between Sharon Springs, Richfield Springs and Cooperstown, those famous resorts of health and pleasure seekers.

It was through the picturesque valley of the Cherry Valley creek, with hills rising on either side, that the Six Nations, from the earliest historic days, had the most important of their trails, the one leading down to their great colony, Oquago, in what is now Broome county, from their settlements along the Mohawk river. This valley, about sixteen miles long and from a quarter of a mile to a mile in width, is nearly fifteen hundred feet above tide water, and its high lands on the eastern side may be justly considered as belonging to the Catskill range of mountains. They terminate abruptly three miles northeast of the village in Mount Independence, whose summit is two thousand feet above the sea. From thence a marvelously beautiful scene is opened, more than a hundred miles in extent. Before one the entire Mohawk valley with large parts of the Adirondack regions is spread out and on a clear day the Green mountains of Vermont can be distinctly seen.

Now as to the wide-spread knowledge of this town. In the old days of stage coaching two important roads met in the little village, one the famous turnpike leading west from Albany, the other the turnpike from the Mohawk river down the Susquehanna valley, following the old Indian trail. Over these roads went the emigrants to the great west, and the cattle and produce from the west went east to the Albany market. Sixty years ago, within the memory of the generation just passing away, Cherry Valley was well known to all travelers on these two routes, and the praise of its old taverns is still sung, not with thirsty memories, I judge, as in 1830 there were twenty-nine licensed places for selling liquor in the village. These same travelers remember, too, that they often saw from thirty to forty "prairie schooners," objects familiar to every one who has traveled in the west, resting over night in the village square.

When the Erie Canal was opened, the first blow was dealt to the prosperity of Cherry Valley; and that was speedily followed by the building of the great Central Railroad, and the line of travel has been entirely changed. Surely we may be forgiven for sounding for awhile the praises of the "good old times." The oldest book in the world is the Egyptian book of the "Maxims of Ptah Hotep," going back as far as the fourth dynasty, about three thousand years before Christ, to a period so remote that everywhere else it is lost in the night of time; and in this book, the same cry is heard, as to the degeneracy of modern times and the glory of those that are gone!

The first classical school west of Albany was established in Cherry Valley, before the revolutionary war, and its advantages in subsequent years brought many people to the village for the purpose of educating their children. At the head of this academy in 1795 was the Rev. Eliphalet Nott, afterwards the distinguished president of Union College and one of the greatest educators our country has ever known. He was the pastor of the little church and combined the duties of teacher with his ministerial labors. Under his management the academy flourished, and in after years continued, through his interest in it, to be a training school for Union College. As one of the college trustees wrote: "Only in rare instances did a young man, fitted for college in that academy, think it possible for him to go elsewhere for an education." To quote from the same writer, W. W. Campbell, "This old Cherry Valley Academy had a peculiar charm for Dr. Nott. He never forgot it; he never ceased to live for it as well as for the people of his first charge. More than half a century later he made a special visit, at the request of the people, to aid in raising funds to enlarge the academy building, and fit it for more extended usefulness. The scene in the church was one never to be forgotten. Dr. Nott, then most venerable in appearance, bearing the dignity of high renown, and far advanced in years, though with intellect still vigorous and unclouded, arose to speak. After looking around for a moment or two, he said, 'I feel to-day that I am like an old soldier, long returned from the wars, and who can only shoulder his crutch and show how fields were won. In looking over this assembly I can see only here and there a gray head, the feeble remnant of those among whom I labored, as preacher and teacher more than fifty years ago. A new generation has come on the stage, with whose liberality in giving, with whose devotion to the cause of learning I am not acquainted; but if I had your fathers as auditors to-day, I should know on whom I could depend.' Such was his opening. The tact as well as feeling of the old man eloquent may readily be seen. The victory was won. Men went out with their purse strings loosened, saying, The money must be raised; and so it was."

    This Cherry Valley Academy, chartered by the Regents in 1796, discontinued in 1865 and again revived, has just been reinstated as a member of the University in good standing. The original parchment charter submitted in its application was signed by John Jay, chancellor, and DeWitt Clinton, secretary, of the Regents in 1796.

    Before the Harvard Law School was opened, when in the north there was only a law school at Litchfield, Connecticut, Cherry Valley had its law school, and the cities of New York and Albany alone had bars equal to that of the little village.   Here lived Jabez D. Hammond, author of "The Political History of New York," Alvan Stewart, the great apostle of abolition, Levi Beardsley, James O. Morse, Isaac Seelye, William W. Campbell, author of "The Annals of Tryon County," who all, as lawyers, judges or authors, had more than local reputation. Many all over our State have heard, too, of the famous Dr. Joseph White, President of the State Medical Society, and his no less well known sons, Delos and Menzo, who all, as physicians and surgeons, achieved great success, and were in many ways in advance of their times in their practice.

These men and many others we have no time to mention, all contributed to the former greatness of the village, but while deploring its changed condition now, we must not fail to speak of the noble support given by its sons to the Union during the war of the rebellion, when the descendants of the revolutionary heroes proved themselves worthy of their parentage on many hard fought battle fields; and, still nobler and harder to do, while languishing in Southern prison pens.

As we look up and down the quiet streets of Cherry Valley and over to the peaceful, everlasting hills, how can we realize what a tragedy was enacted here a little over a hundred years ago, a tragedy which has made the place forever historic ground! In a recent article on the "Border Warfare of the Revolution," Professor John Fiske says: "The village of Cherry Valley in Central New York was destroyed November 11, 1778, by a party of seven hundred Tories and Indians. All the houses were burnt and about fifty of the inhabitants murdered without regard to age or sex. Many other atrocious things were done in the course of the year, but the affairs of Wyoming and Cherry Valley made a deeper impression than any of the others. Among the victims were many refined gentlemen and ladies, well known in the Northern States, and this was especially the case of Cherry Valley.

The Cherry Valley massacre was an event of peculiar interest for several reasons. There had always been the closest friendship between the Indians and the people of this place, and some were even on intimate terms with Joseph Brant, the great Mohawk chief. Indeed, all the land had been bought in the Province of New York from the Indians and no treachery had ever been shown them. Unlike the Wyoming settlement, that of Cherry Valley was on good terms with the neighboring settlements. No civil strife disturbed its peace and prosperity. The massacre was the direct result of the revolutionary war. What causes, then, led to this melancholy result, the destruction of the town and its people; and first, who were these people?

During the religious persecutions of the seventeenth century in England and Scotland, many families went to the north of Ireland where they were at liberty to worship God as they chose. These families were afterwards called Scotch-Irish; and it is interesting for us to know that the late President Anderson's ancestors were among the number. Many of them settled in Londonderry, where some endured the fearful siege in 1689. In the next century a number of the younger generation emigrated to America, and part of them settled in New Hampshire, in a place to which they gave the name of Londonderry. Here they were living when in 1740 the Rev. Samuel Dunlop, an Irishman and a graduate of Trinity College, Dublin, came and told them that he had been offered several hundred acres of land as a gift, in what was then the far west, on condition that he would settle upon it, and induce some of his friends to buy land near and do the same. This land lay in the unbroken wilderness south and west of the settlements along the Mohawk river, which at that time only reached about to the place where the village of Herkimer now stands. "The whole region to the south was untouched by the hand of civilized man until one came to Central Pennsylvania, where the Scotch-Irish Presbyterians and Germans had already settled, and to the westward without limit saving that a few French Jesuits and traders had formed scattered missions and trading posts at Detroit and along the lakes."

Two years before, in 1738, a patent for eight thousand acres of this land had been granted by Lieutenant-Governor Clarke to four men, one of whom was John Lindesay. The next year, Governor Clarke and Mr. Lindesay obtained an assignment of this patent from the others, and after having laid it out in lots, Mr. Lindesay settled on a farm himself and called the place Lindesay's bush. He had doubtless been attracted to the locality by its wild, romantic scenery which reminded him of his native Scotland, but he did not at all appreciate the difficulties of living in a spot so remote from any settlement, and in the first winter, when the snow fell to an unusual depth, he and his family nearly starved to death. Their condition was discovered by an Indian, who came by chance to the house, and who immediately went on his snowshoes to the Mohawk river, twelve miles away, and brought back provisions for them upon his back, and for the rest of the winter he continued to relieve them in the same way. This experience doubtless led to the offer made by Mr. Lindesay to the Rev. Mr. Dunlop and which resulted in about thirty persons with their families, among them David Ramsay, William Gault, James Campbell and William Dickson, moving from New Hampshire in 1741, buying farms and settling down upon them. They were hardy and industrious people, well fitted for the difficult task before them.

When writing some letters soon after, Mr. Dunlop asked Mr. Lindesay where he should date them. On the name of a Scottish town being proposed, Mr. Dunlop, looking down the beautiful valley and on some fine wild cherry trees in blossom, said; "Oh, let us give our place an appropriate name; let us call it Cherry Valley." Soon, on the hillside near Mr. Dunlop's house, was put up a log church, which also did duty as a schoolhouse. In this church was the first English preaching west of the Hudson river. Mr. Dunlop taught the classics to the boys of the settlement and to others who came from the scattering villages on the Mohawk river, and who made their home in his house. It is said that he often guided the plough while listening to the boys scanning Homer and Virgil as they walked in the furrows behind him. Here a number of men were educated who afterwards became very prominent in the Revolution. Mr. Dunlop seems never to have hesitated to undertake anything that he wished to do. Until the year 1745 the Presbyterians in this county referred their ecclesiastical matters to the mother church in Ireland. At that time they formed a Presbytery, and it is said that Mr. Dunlop took the long journey to New Hampshire to attend one of its meeting. Nor was this all. When he left Ireland to seek a home in the new world he was engaged to a young girl, with the condition, however, that if he did not return within seven years she could consider herself at liberty. Now that he had a home for her, he returned to Ireland, knowing that the seven years were almost run out, and that doubtless many were suing for her hand. After making the slow voyage safe from pirates and the dangers of shipwreck, he was delayed in landing and only reached his betrothed the last day of the appointed time to find that she was to be married on the morrow to another man. He claimed his bride, however, and was joyfully accepted as one from the dead, and soon he brought her to his home in the wilderness. It was well for them both that the veil was not lifted from the future, to reveal the sad fate of the gentle lady in 1778.

For about thirty years the settlers of Cherry Valley enjoyed comparative prosperity; fresh men gradually joined their number, one of the most prominent of whom was John Wells, who bought Mr. Lindesay's place, and who, afterwards married a daughter of the Rev. Mr. Dunlop. The church, under its faithful minister's care, prospered, and after a time outgrew the log house, and a frame church was built within the limits of the burying ground which lies near the southern edge of the village. "In this quiet graveyard many a rude slab, split from the limestone ridge hard by, still marks the spot where a pioneer lies wrapt in his long slumber, but whose name no hand skilled with the chisel was there to engrave."

These handy frontiersmen were not only lovers of religion and learning, but were something like the Puritans, of whom it is said that next to going to church they loved to fight. In the French and Indian war, in spite of the dangers surrounding them from the incursions of the Six Nations who were not all loyal to their British allies, all capable of bearing arms were in the army on the British side, and every man became in some sense a soldier. Then, when complaints arose as to the treatment of the colonies by the British crown, no protests were more bold, no resolutions more patriotic than those made in the little valley church in the spring of 1775, ending with these words: "It is our fixed resolution to support and carry into execution everything recommended by the Continental Congress and to be free or die."

There were three members from Cherry Valley in the Committee of Safety of Tryon County, of which John Frey was Chairman. A word as to the limits of Tryon county. This county, taken from Albany county in 1772, was named in honor of William Tryon, then governor of the province. It embraced all that territory in New York state lying west of a line drawn north and south through the center of the present county of Schoharie. The county buildings were at Johnstown, where Sir William Johnson's residence was. In 1784 the name of the county was changed to Montgomery. Its entire population was estimated at ten thousand, of whom not more than twenty-five hundred could have been capable of bearing arms. Now, when we remember that the Six Nations alone, who lived around and among these people, numbered over two thousand brave and skillful warriors, while in the whole department there were over twenty-five thousand savages trained in the use of arms, we will gain a faint idea of what it meant when the yeomen of central New York espoused the cause of liberty.

These three committee men were God-fearing patriots, as the following letter to the committee will show:

CHERRY VALLEY, June 9, 1775.

Sirs:-We received yours of yesterday relative to the meeting of the committee on Sunday, which surprised us not a little, inasmuch as it seems not to be on any alarming circumstance; which, if it was, we should readily attend. But as that does not appear to us to be the case, we think it is very improper; for unless the necessity of the committee sitting, superexceed the duties to be performed in attending the public worship of God, we think it ought to be put off till another day; and therefore we conclude not to give our attendance at this time, unless you adjourn the sitting of the committee until Monday morning; and in that case we will give our attendance as early as you pleases. But otherwise, we do not allow ourselves to be cut short of attending on the public worship, except the case be so neccessitous as to exceed sacrifice. We conclude with wishing success to the common cause and subscribe ourselves the free-born sons of liberty.

JOHN MOORE.
SAMUEL CLYDE.
SAMUEL CAMPBELL.

If you proceed to sit on the Sabbath, please read this letter to the committee, which we think will sufficiently assign our reasons for not attending.

Now, we come to the main cause of the massacre. Before the battle of Oriskany, which battle turned back the tide that threatened the Mohawk Valley with destruction, the Six Nations were persuaded to join the British forces by promises made them of unlimited opportunities for scalping and plunder, and the assurance that they would not have to fight. Instead of this, they met a determined foe, and hand to hand fought for many hours, losing about a hundred of their bravest warriors. They swore vengeance for this loss, and the tale we are to tell of Cherry Valley is one of the results of that bloody 6th of August, 1777.

After General Herkimer was wounded and unable to direct the movements of his army and Colonel Cox was killed, Colonel Campbell of Cherry Valley was in command of the forces and led them off this fatal field. By his side, too, stood another brave officer, Major Clyde from the same place. These prominent acts, and the fact that John Moore of Cherry Valley was a member of the provincial Congress, directed the special attention of the Indians in their plan of revenge, to Cherry Valley. To the Tories, also, the patriotism of this little town was a rebuke, and they hated it, and so were ready to join hands with their savage allies. We can hardly speak with patience about the actions of these same Tories. Some may have been truly anxious to do right, and have thought that they must support their king; but there is no excuse for their dastardly treachery, and their turning to the right and the left upon their neighbors and friends with more than savage cruelty. Again, what can be said of the action of the English government in inciting the murderous attacks of the Indians upon the colonists? To what act in history can it be compared? It is not just, however, historians tell us, to ascribe this wicked dealing to the British commanders in general; it must be charged, they say, to the account of Lord George Germaine and a few unworthy men who were willing to be his tools. "Alone, either the Indians or the Tories would have been comparatively harmless; united, they ranged like fiends over all Tryon county."

Realizing the danger they were in, the people of Cherry Valley in 1777, threw up a rude embankment of logs and earth around Colonel Campbell's house and two large barns which stood on a side hill commanding a full view of the valley. The doors were doubled, strong window shutters were provided, and the whole rendered bullet proof. Two small blockhouses were erected within the enclosure. Here the people gathered and a company of rangers secured their safety during the summer; and in the fall they returned to their homes, as little danger wa to be feared from the Indians during the winter. But in the spring of 1778, General LaFayette was in Johnstown; and he, appreciating the importance of Cherry Valley's position, ordered a fort to be constructed in the town. Before this was build, however, early in May, while the inhabitants were in their old quarters at Colonel Campbell's, Brant planned a descent upon the village with the special object of killing or taking prisoner some of the principal persons, especially the members of the committee, he having been informed truly that it was at that time without a guard of soldiers. Approaching stealthily through the forest from the east he gained the summit of Lady Hill, from which he could look down upon the stockaded house of Colonel Campbell. To his dismay, on the green in from of the house he saw a company of soldiers parading. He abandoned his projected attack, saying to his followers: "Colonel Campbell has got his house well guarded, I see;" only to learn afterwards that he had been deceived by a sight of the boys of the settlement dressed out in paper hats, with wooden weapons, who were thus early practicing the arts of war. Brant withdrew his force to a place on the main road, about two miles to the north, where he himself hid behind a great rock and waited, hoping to learn something definite about the soldiers he had seen and their preparations for defence. This rock is still to be seen, and is called "Brant's Rock." That same day Lieutenant Matthew Wormuth, a militia officer and personal friend of Brant, had come up from the Mohawk river to bring some news about the movements of Colonel Klock and his regiment. As he set out to return home, he was accompanied by a bearer of dispatches, Peter Sitz. As they neared Brant's hiding place, they were challenged by him and ordered to halt. They paid no attention, but spurred their horses on until Lieutenant Wormuth fell, wounded, and his frightened horse turned and rushed back to the village. Brant coming up to his old friend, in his haste tomahawked him with his own hand, mistaking him for a continental officer. Sitz was captured, but managed to destroy the dispatches that gave a true account of the state of the garrison, and gave up a false set which he carried; so Brant went away for that time, and the valley had a short interval of peace.

During the summer the fort was built; it was rude, but sufficient for frontier warfare. The site chosen included the burying ground, and the church itself was used for the headquarters of the troops. The people stored their valuables within its walls, and themselves took refuge there at times. The work was defended by four pieces of artillery and between two and three hundred troops of the Sixth Massachusetts regiment were quartered here under the command of Colonel Ichabod Alden of Danbury, Mass., in whose honor the fort was named.

Within a few years a manuscript journal has been found and published by the Massachusetts Historical Society, that was kept by a Lieutenant William McKendry, of this same Sixth Massachusetts regiment. It is full of interest, beginning as it does at Albany in October, 1777, and closing after the great Sullivan campaign, in January, 1780. His first entry after going to Cherry Valley, July 24, 1778, is as follows: "Arrived at 4 P.M. The regiment was received with much joy, with firing a blunderbuss and one round from the militia and inhabitants, which were posted at Cherry Valley." On the next day he writes: "Drew two days provisions and went to Rev. Mr. Dunlop's and drank sillabub with discoursing the old gentleman about sundries affairs." On the 27th he says: "Begin to board with Mr. James Riches, twenty rods from Fort Alden." On the 6th of August he writes: "The troops moved from Colonel Campbell's to the fort." On the 7th: "Began to build the redout at Fort Alden." On August 25th: "Went to Colonel Campbell's and saw ye Dominie's bee wool breaking;" and so on with accounts of regimental horse races and field days, a wedding and other festivities, as if with no thought of danger.

And indeed it seems as if life might now have gone on safely in the village but for the foolhardiness of Colonel Alden, who, as well as his under officers, presumed too much on the dread the Indians had of artillery and of regular troops. Lieutenant McKendry, as we have seen, had his quarters outside the fort, and the same was true of Colonel Alden, Lieutenant Colonel Stacy, and other officers. On the 6th of November, just as the people were beginning to breathe freely again on account of the approach of winter, news was sent to Colonel Alden from Fort Schuyler of a projected attack on the village within a few days; but even then the Colonel was not aroused to a sense of danger. In vain did Colonels Campbell and Clyde beg him to allow the inhabitants to take shelter in the fort, where there was a plenty of room for them. Colonel Alden said they need fear nothing, that the Indians would never dare to come where there were disciplined troops and that he would send out scouts in every direction.* (See Appendix p 2.)

The people had to be contented, much against their wishes, with the colonel's decision, and that it was not a selfish one is shown by the fact that he still stayed at Mr. Wells's house, on the sloping hillside just below the village with Lieutenant Colonel Stacy and a small guard. It adds to the interest in Mr. Wells's place to know that it was the original "Lindesay's bush," owned and occupied by the first settler, and that in later days, until her marriage and removal to Rochester, it was the home of Mrs. Roswell Hart, whose brother, Mr. Edward Phelon, still lives upon it.

The scouting party sent down the valley was surprised by the Indians and taken prisoners on the night of the 10th of November, and in the early morning hours of the 11th a band of about five hundred Indians and two hundred Tories, under the command of Joseph Brant and Captain Walter Butler, came into the settlement. The snow was several inches deep on the ground and rain falling in the early morning; the atmosphere was thick and hazy, thus helping their designs. Their number was large enough to admit of surrounding each house in which an officer was lodged, and at the same time allowing the main body to attack the fort.

A man coming up the valley on horseback was fired upon and wounded by the Indians. He spurred his horse on up to Mr. Wells's house to alarm Colonel Alden. The colonel was still incredulous, thinking it only a straggling party, and he ordered the guard called in. This delay gave the Indians time to rush by. The advance guard was mostly made up of Seneca Indians, at that time the wildest and most ferocious of any of the Six Nations. Colonel Alden escaped from the house and was pursued down the hill towards the fort by an Indian who called upon him to surrender. This he would not do and turned to fire upon the Indian, but his pistol only snapped. The attempt enraged Brant, for he it was, and he threw his tomahawk at him, and then rushing up, scalped him. Thus the unfortunate officer was the first victim of his sad mistake. Lieutenant-Colonel Stacy was made a prisoner, and every one of the guard was either killed or captured.

The scenes in Mr. Wells's house which the colonel fled from were heartrending. The whole peaceful family was massacred, consisting of Robert Wells, his wife, his mother, four children, his brother and sister and three domestics. The only member of the family to escape was a son, John, who was with an aunt in Schenectady, and who lived to become one of the most distinguished lawyers in New York. This one might, indeed, have said in the words of an English poet:

> "They left of all my tribe
> Nor man, nor child, nor thing of living birth,
> No! not the dog, that watched my household hearth,
> Escaped-that 'morn' of blood upon our plains;
> All perished! I alone am left on earth!
> To whom nor relative nor blood remained,
> No! not a kindred drop that runs in human veins."

A Tory afterward boasted that he killed Mr. Wells at prayer. Rev. Mr. Dunlop's house was about a mile away, and there too the savages were relentless. Mrs. Dunlop, whom we last saw as a happy bride, was killed, and one of her arms thrown into an apple tree. Her husband's and daughter's lives were preserved by a chief called Little Aaron. Even he, however, could not entirely protect the aged man. An Indian in passing seized his hat and ran off with it. Little Aaron followed him to recover it when another Indian attempted to scalp Mr. Dunlop, and was only deterred from his purpose by intense astonishment when the minister's wig came off suddenly. Mr. Dunlop's captivity lasted only a few days, but the shock, grief and exposure had been too much for him and he lived only a few months longer.

On the Clyde homestead, about a mile beyond Mr. Wells's house and on much higher ground, lived the Colonel Clyde of whom I have spoken, with his wife and eight children. Mrs. Clyde was a niece of Matthew Thornton, one of the signers of the Declaration of Independence, and was a very remarkable woman. She had been accustomed in her youth, which was spent in the eastern colonies, to Indian modes of warfare, and had felt with her husband that Colonel Alden was not wise in his feeling of security. The night before the Indian onslaught Mrs. Clyde dreamed three times that the Indians were upon them, and that Molly Brant* (See Appendix p 1.), whom she had once known well, appeared to her and warned her to escape. She was so impressed with the dreams that she aroused her husband and begged him to go once more to the fort and entreat Colonel Alden to allow the people to come within its shelter.

Colonel Clyde started out and had scarcely reached the fort when the attack began. His wife heard the shrieks of her friends, the Wells family, mingled with the hideous Indian war whoops, and then saw a band of savages coming towards her house. She started with her children, one of them an infant, to gain the shelter of the woods. With them went an apprentice boy about sixteen years old and a little dog. In running, the oldest daughter, Agnes, became separated from the rest of the party, and was alone, hidden under a great fallen tree for twenty-four hours. Over the tree passed Indians and Tories, but without discovering her. There was snow on the ground, and the rain which had fallen that morning had turned to sleet, which added to her sufferings, thinly clad as she was. Her mother and the other children went about two miles and there were concealed in the dense woods; but oftentimes the Indians passed by them; at one time one of their guns trailed on the log that covered Mrs. Clyde and her infant. Meantime she saw the smoke from the homesteads burning around her and heard the whoops of the savages as they pursued their diabolical work in one part of the settlement after another, and did not know whether or no the attack on the for was successful

In her case providential circumstances seemed to mock the malice and wrath of men. Her baby did not scream, the little dog did not bark when their enemies were near them, and although they suffered bitterly from exposure and cruel anxiety, the morning of the 12th found them alive, and when the frightened boy went to the fort by a circuitous route, having been warned by his mistress to see if the flag was still flying before venturing near, he was able to tell Colonel Clyde the welcome news of the safety of most of his family.

Colonel Clyde asked the commanding officer for a force to go out with him and bring in his family. The officer said that he would not order any men out on such duty while bands of marauders were still on all sides, but he would call for volunteers. Fourteen brave men offered their services, and led by the boy they went for Mrs. Clyde. She was so benumbed that she could scarcely move, but with help started and walked on bravely, until in passing through Mr. Dunlop's place she saw her murdered friend's arm in the tree. This, with the thought of the fate that might have overtaken her own daughter, threatened to overcome her, but she rallied her forces and pressed on, passing bravely the spot whence she could see the charred, smoking ruins of her own home. A creek in the open meadow was to be crossed before the fort could be reached, and while two men were helping her over the log that served as a bridge, the Indians fired upon the party and some of the shots struck the bridge, but did no harm to them.

About the time of Mrs. Clyde's safe entry into the fort with her family, her daughter Agnes also started from her hiding place. Her progress was through the open fields, and she was repeatedly fired upon. On account of the bitter cold the sentries on the fort had wrapped themselves in blankets. The young girl when she came near enough to see them thus clad, turned to flee again to the wood, thinking that the Indians were in possession of the fort; but she was recognized, and called to come back and at last reached shelter unharmed.

Colonel Campbell was that day at the Mohawk river, but his wife's father and mother, Captain and Mrs. Cannon of Newtown-Martin, were visiting their daughter. As soon as the savages were seen approaching the house, all the negro slaves fled in terror, except one faithful woman who caught up the oldest child, William, ten years old, and hid with him in the garret behind some flax. Captain Cannon was determined to sell his life as dearly as possible, so he took his station behind a tree and fired rapidly at the assailants, until wounded in the leg and taken prisoner by a son of Catrine Montour, who admired the gallant defence of the one old man so much that he spared his life. The following year Catrine Montour, who will be remembered as one of the furies in the awful Wyoming massacre, reproached her son in Mr. Cannon's presence for his humanity, saying, "why did you bring that old man a prisoner? Why did you not kill him when you first took him?"

Mrs. Jane Campbell, her four children and her mother as well as her father were taken prisoners, and the house and barns set on fire. When the negro woman saw the flames she took William down from the garret. At the foot of the stairs stood a Tory, whom the boy recognized in spite of his paint and disguise and called by name. The man said: "That is not my name, but here, pass out this way and run to the woods." Long afterwards, William, who lived to be surveyor general of New York State, and a regent of the university, would tell of the misery of that day when he lay hidden in the forest, and that night when he went through woods and by untrodden ways to the settlements on the Mohawk river. He did not dare to go into any house for fear of meeting enemies instead of friends, but pressed on, hungry, cold, and full of distress at the unknown fate of his mother, brothers and sister, only cheered by the woman, who, when he was ready to drop by the wayside and die from fatigue, urged him on, saying, "When good massa come home, and find missus and de chillun all dead, and the house gone, oh how glad he be to find massa Willie Alive! Come, den, now, less go on; we'll soon git somewhar."

This same woman wrapped the family Bible in a blanket and hid it behind a fence, where it was found after a few days.

When Colonel Campbell hurried home, alarmed by guns fired at the fort, to find only the smoking ruins of his house and no one to tell him the fate of any of his dear ones, who can picture his desolation? The only living thing which he saw as a colt which came running towards him with great joy, kicking up its heels, but falling down dead before it reached him.

It would be too painful to tell all the details of this horrible tragedy, but one more incident may be added to show its character.

Hugh Mitchell, from the field where he was working, saw a party of Indians on the way to his house. As he was too far away to help his family, he fled to the woods for a time, and thus saved his own life. When he returned to his burning house he found the dead bodies of his wife and four children. He first put out the fire, and upon discovering that there was life still in one daughter, about twelve years of age, he took her to the door, and bending over her, sought to restore her to consciousness. Just then another party of savages approached, and he had only time to conceal himself behind a log fence, before their entrance. From his hiding place he saw an infamous Tory, Newberry, with a blow of his hatchet, destroy the last spark of life in his child. The next day, without any assistance, Mr. Mitchell took the dead bodies of his loved ones, on a sled to the fort. Well might Captain Warren exclaim in his journal: "Such a shocking sight my eyes never beheld before of savage and brutal barbarity; to see the husband mourning over his dead wife and four dead children lying by her side, mangled, scalped, and some the head, some the legs and arms cut off, some the flesh torn off their bones by their dogs."*(See Appendix p 2.)

On the 12th of November, the day after the massacre, two hundred militia came from the Mohawk river, but they were too late to do more than disperse the straggling parties of Indians and aid the garrison in their sad duty of bringing in and burying the dead. In the old churchyard a deep trench was dug and there in a common grave most of the martyrs were laid to rest. On the one hundredth anniversary of this day a monument was unveiled in their honor.

The fort, as we have seen, was not taken, and if the inhabitants had only been sheltered there, many valuable lives would have been saved. Lieutenant McKendry in a brief way, says that fourteen men of the 6th Massachusetts regiment were killed and a number taken prisoners; and he gives their names. In all it is estimated that about fifty lost their lives. The principal part of the enemy, with their captives, between thirty and forty in number, spent the night of the 11th about two miles down the valley. "To the prisoners it was a night of wretchedness never to be forgotten. A large fire was kindled, around which they gathered, with no shelter, not even, in most cases, an outer garment to protect them from the storm. There might be seen the old, the infirm and the middle aged, and "Shivering childhood, houseless but for a mother's arms; couchless, but for a mother's breast." Around them gleamed the watch fires of the savages, who were engaged in examining and distributing their plunder. Along up the valley they caught occasional glimpses of the ruins of their dwellings, as some sudden gust of wind or falling timber awoke into new life the decaying flames. An uncertain fate awaited them. If they augured from the scenes they had that day witnessed, it was death. Their minds were filled with fearful foreboding, a secret fear, which one dare not whisper to his fellow, that they might be reserved, as the victims for a more deliberate and dreadful torture."

The morning broke upon a sleepless group; they early resumed their march down the Cherry Valley creek, divided into small companies. This day Brant made another attack on the fort, but was repulsed, and concluded to give up the attempt to carry it. On the 13th, joy filled the hearts of the captives on learning that Brant had decided to send back the women and children. This was accordingly done, except in the case of Mrs. John Moore and her children, and Mrs. Colonel Campbell and her four children, who were told that they must go to the land of the Senecas with their captors on account of the active part their husbands had taken. As soon as the prisoners returned to the fort and joined those who had escaped, it was decided to abandon the settlement. Most of them moved to the Mohawk Valley, and there, until the close of the war, did noble service. The garrison remained in the fort until the following June.

In Lieutenant McKendry's journal mention is made from month to month of dead bodies found in the woods or men who died in camp from the effect of wounds received the day of the massacre. I think the exact number of the killed on that day will never be known. He also records various alarms given of hostile Indians in the neighborhood. Other foes came, now that the place was deserted. On April 5th, 1779, he says: "One of the soldiers killed a wolf." On May 5th he notes, "Some squall of snow to-day;" and on Jun 3rd,

"A very hard frost last night which killed the blossoms at this place." On the 18th of June the regiment left the fort and marched to Otsego lake to join General James Clinton's division of Sullivan's army. Soon after, a band of marauders set fire to the church and so the last vestige of the place was destroyed.

The hand of retributive justice soon overtook the Tory Newberry, who was convicted the year following on the testimony of Hugh Mitchell and hung as a murderer.

In 1781 Captain Walter Butler, the real author of the massacre, suffered the very fate he had so often meted out to others. Fleeing up the Mohawk river, after a disastrous defeat at Johnstown, he swam his horse across the West Canada creek and then turned to face his pursuers. An Oneida Indian, whose rifle ball brought him wounded to the ground, cast aside his gun and blanket and crossed the stream. His answer to Butler's beseeching cry for mercy, was only; "Sherry Valley, remember Sherry Valley," and a cut with his tomahawk that cleft his skull. The place is called still Butler's ford.

On the other hand, Joseph Brant, or Thayendanegea, whose remarkable career deserves an extended notice, lived in Canada many years after the massacre, where he was honored by the British government. From Brantford, Ontario, named for him, the following dispatch was sent a few years ago to the New York Tribune: "A monument to Joseph Brant, Chief of the Six Nations, who was chiefly instrumental in securing the adherence of the Six Nations to the British cause in the Revolutionary War, was unveiled here to-day. It was erected by the Six Nation Indians of the Mohawk village near Brantford. The center piece is a heroic figure of Brant, nine feet high. At either side of the Cornish gray granite pedestal are groups of three figures each, representing chiefs of the Mohawk, Tuscarora, Oneida, Seneca, Onondaga and Cayuga tribes."

Any comment upon this is unnecessary.

We will now go back to the Indians and their captives. As Mrs. Campbell's mother, Mrs. Eleanor Cannon, could not keep up with the Indians in their march, one of them tomahawked her, before her daughter's eyes, and left her body by the wayside. The same Indian drove Mrs. Campbell along with his bloody, uplifted hatchet and threatened her with a like fate if she lagged behind, carrying as she did an infant son of eighteen months. Just after Mrs. Cannon's awful death, Mrs. Campbell saw an Indian tear a baby from its mother's embrace, dash its brains out against a tree and cast its body on one side. Soon another savage approached Mrs. Campbell and without saying anything took her child away and disappeared with him in the forest. She said to herself: "That Indian is more merciful than the other one and has taken my boy so far away that I cannot hear his screams when he kills him." All day she marched on, her heart full of grief, but at night when tired and footsore she reached the camping ground, the first thing she saw was her boy in the Indian's arms, and he was being fed and warmed by the great fire. All the rest of the long way this same Indian carried her child, bringing his to his mother at night.

They marched between two and three hundred miles, during the rest of the dreary month of November. Their route was down the Susquehanna river to its junction with the Tioga river, thence up the Tioga to a place near its source, thence across to the head of Seneca lake and along its eastern shore to the Indian castle and village of Kanadesaga, a few miles from the present village of Geneva. Here all of their children were taken from Mrs. Moore and Mrs. Campbell, not even excepting the infant, and given to different families among different tribes of Indians. Mrs. Campbell was then given to a family in Kanadesaga to take the place of one who had recently died. It was composed of squaws, with the exception of one old warrior, who could no longer hunt or go on the war path. In their smoky hut, destitute of every comfort, the first winter of her captivity was passed. Some one said to her afterwards: "How could you live through all this?" "Oh," said she, "one can't always die when one longs for death." As soon as she recovered her strength a little, she began with great tact to make herself very useful to the members of the household, and little by little she gained many privileges. The squaws were ignorant of the most common arts of life, and she sewed for them and also made garments for the families near them who in return gave them corn and venison.

There was only one kettle in which to cook everything, and the hut boasted of one broken plate and one spoon. Mrs. Campbell persuaded the women to let her do the cooking also, and thus ensured the cleanliness of the food; and they, perceiving after a time what her wishes would be, allowed her to help herself first, on the plate, before putting their hands into the kettle in true savage fashion. She was also allowed to stop working on Sunday, when she told them how sacred that day was to her,* (By means of a notched stick she had been able to keep the count of the days, and so knew when Sunday came.) and in many ways they showed her kindness.

She had no change of clothing, and it was with difficulty that she could wash and mend her few garments, wrapped meanwhile in blankets. Towards spring the British officers at Fort Niagara learned that there was a white captive at Kanadesaga, who needed clothing, and they sent a man on horseback to the village with a bundle for her. Something having been said one day about her cap, an Indian said to her: "Come to my house and I will give you a cap." Her adopted mother motioned her to follow him. When she went into the hut, the man pulled a cap from behind a beam and gave it to her, saying in English: "I got that cap in Cherry Valley. I took it from the head of a woman." To her horror, she recognized it as one belonging to her friend, Jane Wells, and knew that the man was her murderer. The little cap was stained with blood and had a cut in the crown made by his tomahawk. She kept it carefully and was able afterwards to give it to a cousin of Miss Wells.

The last time that the great Indian festival and sacrifice of the "White Dog" was celebrated in Kanadesaga was during her residence there.

Meanwhile Colonel Campbell had been doing all in his power to effect his family's release, aided by his friends, Governor Clinton and General Schuyler. In the spring of 1779, he was able to send an Indian messenger to Colonel John Butler at Fort Niagara to tell him that the latter's proposition had been accepted by our government, and that Mrs. Butler and her children would be allowed to join General Butler in Canada as soon as Mrs. Campbell and all her children were safely returned.

When the Indians adopt prisoners in place of dead relatives, they are very reluctant to give them up. Colonel Butler was obliged to go himself to Kanadesaga to plead for Mrs. Campbell's release. A council was called and as near relatives in the Genesee village had to be consulted, the old Seneca king, Guyanguahta, or Grahta, offered to be the messenger and go on foot to ask their consent. He had always been kind to Mrs. Campbell, and when he brought her the welcome news of his successful mission, he said to her, " You are now going home and I rejoice. If I live till the war is over, I will come and see you." Soon after the old king's return Mrs. Campbell was taken to Fort Niagara in the Seneca village of Niagara, near the present site of Youngstown. Over the trail from Kanadesaga she went, and whether she passed the site of Avon and descending into the valley of the Genesee crossed the river a few miles above the Avon bridge, or whether she was with the party of Butler's rangers who were known to have crossed the Genesee river at its mouth, I do not know, but for many years my interest in driving past these fertile fields of Western New York and through our valley, well named Genesee, or the beautiful, has been heightened by the thought that I was passing over the very ground once trodden by my great grandmother in her captivity, long before the white man had made his home here.

In Fort Niagara Mrs. Campbell spent about a year, treated as a British prisoner of war. Rations were given here from the government supplies, but as she desired to buy clothing and some comforts not provided, she made linen shirts for the officers with fine ruffles on the bosoms and cuffs, being paid by them the price of a yard of linen for making one. From crying so much and from the smoke of the Indian hut her eyes had become almost useless, so the officers presented her with a pair of spectacles, which she used while a prisoner and for some little time afterwards. After laying them aside she was unable to see out of the spectacles again until she was nearly ninety. She was thirty-four years old at the time of her captivity.

Meanwhile Colonel Butler was instituting a very diligent search for the four children. It would have been doubtles impossible to recover them but for the fact that the

Indians were driven into Fort Niagara on account of General Sullivan's successful expedition against them.

In that day these western clearings were not only the home of large bodies of Indians whence they made forays on the defenceless in all parts of the country, but they were the great sources of supply for savages in the eastern as well as the western part of the colony. Corn in great quantities grew here, and remains of many orchards are still to be found. For these reasons Sullivan's soldiers were justified in their relentless work of devastation, laying the country waste as they did for an extent of nearly two hundred miles. Until his campaign the Indian power over this whole region of country was supreme.

After many months Mrs. Campbell was sent to Montreal with her daughter and two of her sons. One of these two boys had been adopted by an Indian chief, who tried to hide him away from Butler's rangers, and when he came back his dress was ornamented with two breast pins which had no doubt been taken from some captive.

The other son, James, my grandfather, who was six years old when the massacre took place, was not found for a long time. He had been placed with a branch of the Mohawk tribe, living at Caughnawaga, the Indian village that is still to be seen in passing down the St. Lawrence river, the place where the steamers used to take on the Indian pilot, Jean Baptiste. James was very happy in his captivity, being kindly treated by all, and learning many things from the Indians, forgetting, however, the English language. He was adopted into a family by the name of Williams, and one of his playmates was the father of Eleazer Williams, who is thought by some to have been the lost dauphin of France, the son of Louis XVI and Marie Antoinette. He was delighted with the making of maple sugar and with fashioning "mococks," the little birch bark baskets which the Indians filled with the sugar. He was working busily on some of these "mococks" the morning that a party of Colonel Butler's rangers found him, and when urged to go to Montreal with them, he refused entirely, until bribed with the promise of being dressed in a suit of rifle green like their own uniforms. When he reached Montreal, Mrs. Butler took him into a great room where his mother was. Besides her there were many wives of English officers and other ladies. Mrs. Campbell was asked not to say anything in order to see whether or no James would remember her. He was told to go and sit down by any lady he chose, and to his mother's great joy, the little fellow soon went to her side, and although he could not understand what she said to him, he showed plainly that he remembered her.

At Montreal they were kept waiting for several months for their discharge as prisoners of war, and for the other exchanged prisoners. At last they set out on their journey home. Several young ladies from Albany, who were in boarding school in Montreal when the war broke out, and had been unable to return home hitherto, were placed under Mrs. Campbell's care. They were taken to Lake Champlain and put on a cartel boat. As they were nearing the end of their journey, by mistake the boat was fired upon. Mrs. Campbell said that nothing in her whole experience had been more dreadful to her than the thought of again being captured, when she and her children were so near their home and safety. When the alarm occurred and it was feared that the boat would not be allowed to proceed, Mrs. Campbell and her party were landed and put in charge of Colonel Ethan Allen. Colonel Allen told them that they should not again fall into the enemy's hands, so putting them on horseback, he sent them across the country to Albany, escorted by a hundred men. Here great kindness was shown Mrs. Campbell, and she was soon joined by her husband after a two years' separation. Then they went up the river to where West Troy is situated, where they lived until the spring of 1784, when they returned to Cherry Valley.

Here they began life anew, only their land being left to them. They took with them various articles of household furniture, among others a tall clock which was bought with the warrants issued to Colonel Campbell for his services during the Revolutionary War. Mrs. Campbell had brought pear and apple seed with her from Canada, and some of the trees that grew from these seeds are still on the place.

Colonel Campbell built a log house on the site of his old home, and here during the summer he and his wife entertained over night General Washington, Governor Clinton and some distinguished officers of their party who were with them. They came up the valley to see the site of the massacre and went from there to Otsego lake. Mrs. Campbell gave her guest tea out of doors under an apple tree whose trunk is still standing covered with vines. The next morning General Washington spoke of Mrs. Campbell's sons and she said to him: "I will give them to my country's service whenever they are needed." But the general answered that they had seen so much of war and its miseries that he hoped peaceful days were before them now. One family after another came back to their old homes, and little by little the settlement was rebuilt. It is interesting to note that the Clyde family, whose narrow escape we have mentioned, occupied again their farm, and that it is still, as well as the Campbell farm, in possession of descendants of the same name.

One of the first acts of the people, as a whole, was to call the members of the old congregation together in the "meeting-house" yard, to choose trustees to look after the temporalities of the church, in accordance with a recent law passed by the legislature for the help of congregations situated like themselves. The call is dated March 19, 1785, and begins thus: "We, the ancient inhabitants of Cherry Valley, having returned from exile finding ourselves destitute of our church officers," and so on. What a scene the first meeting of the people must have been! As they stood about the blackened ruins of their old church, near the grave where so many of their kinsmen and friends were buried, without a pastor, without elders or deacons, they must indeed have felt like returned exiles. By 1790 they succeeded in erecting a new building, of the barest possible description, however, if we can believe the testimony of a traveler who on seeing it said, that "he had many times seen the house of God, but never before had he seen the Lord's barn."

To return for a few moments to Colonel and Mrs. Campbell. They spent many happy years on the old homestead, living to see their children's grandchildren. One of their grand-daughters, Mrs. Turner, still remembers visiting them when a child, and says that her grandfather would go out early in the morning to attend to his farm, and about eleven o'clock would come into the house, take a glass of bitters, and then sit down and read aloud to his wife while she was spinning flax on her little wheel. She remembers their great interest in Scott's novels as they came out.

Colonel Campbell died in 1824, but his widow survived him twelve years. His character through life was irreproachable, and for many years he was a consistent professor of Christianity. The same grand-daughter says, too, that it was not until within a few months of her death that her grandmother's erect frame showed any sighs of age or her face any wrinkles. To the last months of her life she would drive over the steep hills to Cooperstown to visit her youngest son, Robert Campbell, Esq., whose beautiful home on the shores of Otsego lake is still occupied by his daughter, Mrs. Turner, and while there would visit old friends who could talk over the days of the war, who, like herself had gone through many trials and privations. In "Women of the Revolution," Mrs. Ellet says of her: "She was the last survivor of the Revolutionary women in the region of the head waters of the Susquehanna. Her later days, to the close of a life marked with so much of active enterprise and stirring incident, were days of industry. Like the Roman matron, she bore the distaff in her hand, and sat with her maidens around her, and her characteristic energy was infused into everything she did. Her memory unimpaired, she was a living chronicle of days gone by, the peculiar circumstances in which she was placed during the war having brought her into personal acquaintance with almost all the prominent men engaged on both side. The feminine and domestic virtues that adorned her character, rendering her beloved in every relation, were brightened by her unaffected piety. It was the power of Christian principle that sustained her through all her wanderings and trials, and in a lonely captivity among a barbarous people. It was this which cheered and supported her when, on the verge of a century, having survived the companions who had commenced life with her, surrounded by her children, and her descendants to the fourth generation, she passed calmly to her rest."

James S. Campbell, the son who succeeded to the farm, lived there until his ninety-eight year, seeing his seven sons and one daughter grow up to manhood and womanhood. On the sixtieth anniversary of his wedding day, an unbroken family circle, they gathered at the old homestead. When he was over eighty, just seventy-five years after his release, he went with his son, Judge William W. Campbell, to the old

Indian village Caughnawaga, where he had been a captive, and tried to find some one who would remember him. It was pathetic to hear him tell that he felt like a veritable Rip Van Winkle when he found only one woman who remembered hearing her grandfather talk about the old times. His adopted mother was still living, but was away on a visit among the St. Regis Indians. There was only one stone building that was familiar to him, the cottage where he had lived. During the war of the Rebellion, although an old man, his interest and patriotism were remarkable, and his eyesight was so good that he was able to read all the newspapers, and study the maps of the seat of war. He used to say, in speaking of the sufferings of one of his grandsons in rebel prisons: "Oh, the Indians were not so cruel as are the Southerners to their captives." When the war closed and General Grant came to Albany to take part in the great celebration there of the national victory, Mr. Campbell was visiting a son who lived on the banks of the Hudson river near the city. The committee in charge of the ceremonies sent for him and asked him to sit on the platform with other distinguished guests. At this time he was ninety-three years old. He had quite a conversation with General Grant, who manifested much interest in the old man, and in the fact that he was talking with one who in his youth was a prisoner in the Revolutionary War, and who remembered talking, after that war was over, in his own home, with General Washington.

APPENDIX

[I.]

Since writing this paper, the following letter has been received:

Buffalo, N.Y., December 9, 1890.

WM. F. PECK, Esq., Secretary of the Rochester Historical Society:

Dear Sir - Some two years ago I chanced to get access to a mass of papers relating to colonial and revolutionary times, which were preserved by the descendants of Col. Daniel Claus, at Niagara, Canada. Among them was a letter dictated by the famous Molly Brant to Col. Claus, announcing the departure of the expedition to Cherry Valley. It was written from Niagara, and stated that the "Old King," or Sayengueraghta, was in command. He was the ruling sachem of the Senecas, and led the Indians at Wyoming. I think the letter has never been printed, and that the author of the paper to be read on Friday evening, may like to see it. The letter was written in the Mohawk tongue, and was translated, a few years since, by my Indian friend, Isaac Bearfoot. Claus, you will remember, was a son-in-law of Sir William Johnson, and a trusted servant of the crown. I have always known that the tradition of the Brant family and the Mohawks generally, affirmed that Brant was not the leader on that occasion; that on his return journey from the Mohawk Valley, he met the expedition by chance, and was persuaded by Butler and the Old King to turn back with them, together with a small band of his Mohawk followers, and that he exerted himself to restrain the ferocity of the Senecas and Tories. My adopted Indian mother, Catharine Johns, the daughter of Brant, so understood the facts. Although an American, I think Brant has not been justly dealt with by our historians, although Col. Stone has probably erred in painting the old chief in too softened and flattering colors.

I send a copy of the letter referred to, as it, in some sense, confirms the family tradition. Mrs. Johns, by the way, never heard of the letter in her lifetime, and none of the family descendants, to my knowledge, know of its existence.

Yours very truly,
WM. C. BRYANT.

MY ELDER BROTHER:

I received just now a letter from Miss Mary Deyonwadonti[1] Niagara. She says: Tell the governor that I have heard that Oraghgwatrihon[2] is coming back again. She says, I want to hear what happened to his band who were with him on the lake. She says, Governor Asharekowa[3] I greet, and thank him much for what he did. His message is here at Niagara. His words are pleasant. Tell him, therefore, that the people of the Long House are much gratified. She ways, we are now awaiting what will happen to the whole Long House. About 500 left here Oct. 28th for Karitongeh.[4] They said in 8 days Karitongeh shall be destroyed. Sakayeugwaraghdon[5] is their leader.

To Col. Claus, Montreal, I, John Deserontyon[6] have written this.

Dec. 3, 1778.

[II.]

[From Sparks's MSS in Harvard College Library.
Extract from Capt. Benj. Warren's Diary,
Cherry Valley, 1778.]

About the first of November Gen. Hand, who was ordered to the command of the Northern Department, came to direct us to determine on the expediency of quartering troops here during the winter. He called for a return of what ordnance stores, ammunition, etc., I had in the garrison; meanwhile an express arrived from Fort Stanwix, informing that one of the Oneidas was at a Council of war of the enemy's, in which it was determined to visit Cherry Valley. The General had the regiment turned out and reviewed them; he payed us a high compliment in orders and in consequence of the express, he went down and ordered Col. Klock to send us immediately 200 men to re-inforce us, which the Gen. wrote, was to have been here the 9th of November and ordered up a large quantity of provisions and ammunition store, which, however, did not come to hand nor any reinforcement of men, and on Wednesday, the 11th, about 12 o'clock, the enemy to the number of 650, rushed upon us, surrounded headquarters and the fort immediately and pushed vigorously for the fort, but our soldiers behaved with great spirit and alertness, defended the fort and repulsed them, after three hours and a half smart engagement. Col. Alden in endeavoring to reach the fort was killed; Col Stacy made prisoner together with Lieut. Holden, Ensign Garrett, the Surgeon's mate, and a Sergeant, about 12 or 14 of the regiment; twelve of the regiment beside the Col. killed and two wounded.

November 12th.-No reinforcements till about 9 or 10 o'clock. The Indians came on again and gave a shout for rushing on, but our cannon played on them brisk; they soon gave way; they then went round the settlement, burnt all the buildings, mostly the first day, and collected all the stock and drove the most of it off, killed and captivated all the inhabitants, a few that hid in the woods excepted, who have since got into the fort.

November 13th.-In the afternoon and morning of the 13th we sent out parties after the enemy withdrew; brought in the dead; such a shocking sight my eyes never beheld before of savage and brutal barbarity: to see a husband mourning over his dead wife with four dead children lying by her side, mangled, scalped, and some their heads, some their legs and arms cut off, some torn the flesh off their bones by their dogs- 12 of one family all killed and four of them burnt in his house.

Saturday, 14th.-The enemy seemed to be gone. We sent out to collect what was left of cattle or anything; found some more dead, and buried them.

Sunday, 15th.-This day some provisions arrived, being the first supply after the first attack, when we had not a pound of bread for man in garrison, for 4 or 5 days, but a trifle of meat. In the afternoon a scout, we thought, had been taken by them, a sergeant and with arrives in sage. By some they took prisoners they let go again informed they had a number wounded and we saw a number of them fall, so that we have reason to think we killed more of them than they killed of our regiment, though they butchered about 40 women and children, that has been founded. It came on to storm before the engagement began, first with rain, but for this day past it has been a thick snow storm.

[III.]

[From Boston Gazette and Country Journal,
Monday, Dec. 7, 1778.]

From an officer who was in the fort at Cherry Valley, November 11th, when it was attacked, we have the following account, viz:

On Saturday night, 8th November, an express arrived from Fort Stanwix, informing them that an Oneida Indian had acquainted them that he sat in Council in the Seneca Country with the Six Nations, and other tribes, and that they had concluded to attack Fort Alden, in Cherry Valley. On Sunday morning a sergeant and 12 men were sent on the road by Beaver Dam, towards the enemy, to continue five days; another scout with a non-commission officer and five men, were sent on the road to Springfield, to continue four days;; these tow roads being the only avenues from the enemy's country to this place, except an old Indian path which had been neglected by us; at the same time we sent by the same roads, scouts in the morning, which returned at night. On Wednesday, the 11th, it rained very hard; the enemy came by the above-mentioned path, past by two houses, and lodged themselves in a swamp, a small distance back of Mr. Wells's house, headquarters. * * * * *

The fort was commanded after Colonel Alden's death by the brave Major Whiting of Dedham, and the two cannons under the direction of the brave Capt. Hickling of this town, who was chief engineer in building the fort, and whose assistance contributed in saving of it.

[From Boston Gazette and Country Journal, Jan. 4, 1779.]

POUGHKEEPSIE, DEC. 14.

Extract of a letter from Tryon County, Nov. 24, 1778:

SIR-I have had no opportunity to give you an earlier account of the destruction at Cherry Valley, where I arrived the day after the tragedy was acted, and did not return home till last night, having been busied in collecting and burying the dead, and getting the distressed inhabitants brought off. I was never before spectator of such a scene of distress and horror.

*   *   *   *

Of the wretched surviving inhabitants, there are 182 who have neither house nor home, nor a morsel of bread; are almost naked, and a great part of them without a penny to purchase any of the necessaries of life. And in all this massacre there were but 3 men of the place killed, all the rest being helpless women and children. *   *   *   *   *

You may depend on this as fact, and as near as I could possibly collect the particulars of this doleful affair, wherein I have a sister and her amiable daughter carried off by the enemy.

M. R.

NOTES:
1. Mary Brant, or Deyonwadonti-"Many opposed to one."
2. Oraghgwatrihon-A young officer and friend of Molly.
3. Gov. Asharekowa-Gov. Haldimand, "Big Sword."
4. Karitongeh (Cherry Valley)-"Place of the oaks."
5. The usual Mohawk orthography of Old King's name or title, meaning "Disappearing Smoke."
6. Deserontyon-"Capt. John" or Deseronto, meaning "The lightning has struck."

CHERRY VALLEY AT THE TIME OF THE MASSACRE.

Chapter III from
History of Cherry Valley

At the time of the Massacre the Fort and the village of Cherry Valley,--if it may be called a village, comprising as it did only half a dozen houses and a church,--was situated in and around the present Cemetery at the lower end of the village and at the upper end of a valley, resembling a Roman Amphitheater in shape; being, apparently, about six miles in length by one mile in width, and surrounded on all sides by gracefully sloping, wooded hills. As a strict matter of fact the valley continues to the South, until it joins the larger valley of the Susquehanna, but it turns sharply to the right where the Westford hills rise, a mile or two below the village of Roseboom, and is so hidden from view by the hills that it appears to end with them. The hills to the North of the village over-look the Mohawk Valley; the streams on that side seeking the Ocean by way of the Mohawk, while those on the South side mingle with the waters of the Susquehanna. Some older geographers have contended that the latter river has its source in the Cherry Valley hills instead of in Otsego Lake.

On the hill at the upper end of the valley, in a direct line from the Fort stood the log house of Col. Samuel Campbell, on the site of the residence now occupied as a summer home by his great-great-grand-children; a half mile to the east and on the same level was the house and shop of James Moore, the blacksmith of the settlement, on the lands now owned by Elisha Flint, and North of him lived a Nelson family. About the same distance to the North of Col. Campbell's was the home of his father-in-law, Matthew Cannon, (disputed); while at an equal distance to the West, was the home of John Campbell, now the summer home of the writer. The present Jackson Millson farm was then occupied by a James Campbell.

On the road to the West, leading to Springfield, lived the Rev. Samuel Dunlop at the foot of Livingston's Glen, on the lands of Mrs. A. B. Cox. There is a tradition that further up the Glen there was a sort of flax or carding mill, in which lived the family of the owner, whose name is not given. Following the Springfield road: the McClellans occupied the present Chauncey Steenburgh farm; James and William Campbell the Fred Blumenstock farm; the Coonrads, the farm now owned by Richard Bierman; the Culleys the farm now occupied by C. W. Sherman and the Shanklands the Elijah Bush farm; Capt. M'Kean lived on the James Horton place and had the M'Kowns as neighbors. The Wiggy Willsons, so called from the fact that the head of the family wore a wig, to distinguish them from the other Willson family, lived in Irish Hollow.

The Wells lived on a knoll about a third of a mile South of the Fort, on the present Phelon farm, and on the hill to the West, on the farm now owned by a descendant, Capt. James D. Clyde, was the home of Major Clyde. Further on were the McKellips on the present James Wikoff farm. Down the valley to the South of the Wells lived the Gaults on the Frank Campbell farm and the Dicksons on the present Mrs. George Head farm. On the opposite side of the valley, on the farm now occupied by a descendant, Louis G. Willson, lived John and James Willson, and South of them the Scotts, on the Wikoff farm.

Nearly opposite the Fort, on the East side of the valley, lived the Thompsons, on the knoll near the Sulphur Spring; further North, John Foster, on the farm now owned by E. L. Hinckley. Near the present Reservoir was the house and Saw Mill of Hugh Mitchell and, beyond, on the Marks farm, lived Patrick Davidson. Still further North, on the Dewitt C. Campbell farm, was the house of a family named Coons. John Moore, tradition says, lived on the Elisha Moore farm a little over two miles East of the village, but it seems more probable that he should have erected his house on the hill to the West, over-looking the Mohawk Valley, now owned by William H. Waldron.

A further list might be given but this is sufficient to show the limits of the Massacre. It will be seen that the limits of what was known as the Cherry Valley settlement were, on the West and South, almost identical with the boundaries of the present Town of Cherry Valley in those directions. To the East and North the boundaries were not much different than at present, but the Indians either did not reach the more distant houses, or the owners had sufficient warning so that they escaped to the Mohawk settlements.

At the time of the Massacre most of the male inhabitants of Cherry Valley, over the age of sixteen, were serving in the Continental Army, at distant points. At first thought it seems strange that the men who had lived all their lives among the Indians and knew all their wiles and strategems, and were thoroughly acquainted with their methods of warfare, should have been sent to the main armies and men unacquainted with the ways of the Indian be sent to protect a frontier settlement. It can only be explained on the theory that experience had shown that when men were left to protect their home settlements, their zeal for the cause of patriotism was likely to be lost sight of in their desire to look first after their own interests and the improvement of their farms and material prospects. In the case of Cherry Valley, it was a sad mistake. Had such men as Capt. M'Kean, Col. Campbell and Col. Clyde been at home, it is safe to say, the Indians would not have found the settlement so unprepared, and that many of the lives lost in that horrible butchery would have been saved.

Among the men who, by their ability, prominence, or zeal for the cause of patriotism, gave honor to Cherry Valley during the Revolutionary period, the first place must be given to the Rev. Samuel Dunlop, by reason of his age, great learning and the position he had so long occupied in the settlement. His great age prevented him from taking active part in the conflict but his advice was sought by all on matters pertaining to the war, and the patriotism displayed by the inhabitants of this section was largely due to his influence.

John Moore was the most prominent resident of the place during this period, though not distinguished as a soldier, owing to his lameness. He was a delegate to the first, second, third, fourth and fifth Provincial Congresses; a member of the State Committee of Safety, and several times a Member of Assembly.

Capt. M'Kean, though not an educated man, was one of the leading men of the settlement by reason of his natural abilities and physical strength and endurance. In such times physique and agility were quite as important as mental training, and indeed were likely to give the possessor greater prominence. M'Kean was accounted one of the most skillful Indian fighters in the country. He had commanded a company of Rangers in the French war, and also during the Revolution. During the war he was raised to the rank of Major. He was killed in the battle of Durlock, near Sharon Springs, in the summer of 1781.

Samuel Clyde, who was raised to the rank of Col., early in 1778, was one of the most prominent men and active patriots of the settlement. It is claimed that, after the death of Gen. Herkimer, the Officers wished to elect him Brigadier General in the place of Herkimer, but that he declined, on the ground that his advancement over the heads of Officers of higher rank, would cause jealousies which would be injurious to the American cause. The failure to appoint a successor to Gen. Herkimer is said to have been due to this refusal on the part of Mr. Clyde, who was then a Major. Col. Clyde was a member of the State Assembly in 1777-8, and Sheriff of Montgomery County in 1785-9.

Col. Samuel Campbell was one of the leaders of the settlement in all matters--social, religious, political and military. He was a member of the Tryon County Committee of Safety and a Col. of the Tryon County Minute Men. His grand-son, the late Judge W. W. Campbell, author of the "Annals of Tryon County," states that as the highest Officer left in command, he led off the troops after the Battle of Oriskany. Col. Campbell was the intimate friend of Gov. Clinton, and numbered among his friends most of the public men of the North. As late as 1802 he was a member of Assembly from Tryon County.

James and John Willson were among the leading and most influential residents. The Rev. Mr. Swinnerton, in his "Historical Sketch of the Presbyterian Church of Cherry Valley," states that the former was, in 1739, High Sheriff of Albany County, which then included all this part of the country. He came here first in that year, as a surveyor, in company with Mr. Lindesay, and later on settled here. He was Commissary for the regiment stationed in the Fort.

The Wells were the social leaders of this part of the Country. John Wells, who died just previous to the Revolution, was a King's Magistrate and his son Robert Wells, was a Major in the Tryon County Militia. The entire Wells family were killed in the Massacre, except a son who was in Schenectady at the time. The latter was afterwards the famous New York lawyer--John Wells.

James Cannon, although a young man, was a very active patriot and afterwards became a man of considerable importance in Otsego County, holding several County offices.

Hugh Mitchell and Thomas Shankland, though men of inferior eduction and social position, were nevertheless, by reason of their activity and patriotism, men of some consideration in the settlement. The former was, in 1775, a member of the Schenectady Committee of Safety. Thomas Spencer, the Indian interpreter, was also for a time a resident of Cherry Valley. He rendered valuable services to the Americans during the Revolution.

There were a number of others who, by reason of their activity in the cause of Liberty, are worthy of mention, but the above list comprises those who might be termed the "leading men" in the settlement. It is a remarkable list for a little frontier settlement of three hundred people. Not alone because of the prominence of those mentioned, in the affairs of the western part of the Province, but also for the reason that so many of them were men of excellent social standing and superior education.-- To the latter facts the former was doubtless due.-- The Dutch of the Mohawk Valley though an excellent, sturdy and honest people, were not, as a rule, an educated class, and they readily yielded precedence to the brighter and more cultivated intellects of the Cherry Valley leaders, in their councils and deliberations, nowithstanding the fact that each district was, in military matters, very tenacious of its rights.

It is interesting in this connection to note that many of the men who were the most prominent during the Revolution and the years following, in the affairs of the Mohawk Valley, received their early education at Rev. Mr. Dunlop's school in Cherry Valley. The most notable of these was John Frey, for many years the most prominent resident of the Valley.

THE FINAL DESTRUCTION OF THE SETTLEMENT.

Chapter VI from
History of Cherry Valley

Although the greater part of the inhabitants of Cherry Valley sought more protected places of residence, immediately after the Massacre, a few hardy settlers still clung to their homes, doubtless in the belief that there was so little in the way of plunder left to repay them that the Indians would not make another attack, or perhaps, in this poverty, dreading more the seeking of new homes among a strange people than the chance of an attack from the Indians.

Only two incidents of especial moment occurred during the early winter following the Massacre.-- The first was the killing, by the Indians, of John Thompson, a son of Alexander Thompson, a resident of Cherry Valley, who had fled to the Mohawk at the time of the Massacre. Young Thompson, who was a promising youth of about twenty, had started to ride up from the Mohawk with a party of young men, to visit his former home. When at almost the identical spot at which Lieut. Wormuth (the early spelling of this name seems to have been Wormwood) was slain, they were fired upon by a party of Indians and Thompson was instantly killed. The remainder of the party escaped.

The other incident which occasioned considerable talk at the time, was the hanging of Wiggy Willson. Willson's sympathies were known to be with the Tories and he was suspected by the settlers of acting as a spy on the settlement. At about the time of the killing of young Thompson, and perhaps in consequence of that act, the garrison became suspicious that the Indians contemplated another attack on the settlement. It was thought that Wiggy Willson might be able to give information regarding the intentions of the Indians. Accordingly a party, composed of settlers and soldiers, visited him and demanded that he should inform them as to the intentions of his red friends. Unfortunately for himself he could not give the desired information; doubtless for the reason that he was as ignorant of the matter as his neighbors. The latter had, however, little faith in Wiggy's sincerity, and believing that a little "moral suasion" was needed, produced a rope and in a moment he was swinging from a convenient appletree. Leaving him thus suspended a sufficient length of time to convince him of their earnestness, and to give him a fair idea of the unpleasantness of that means of ending life, he was let down to the ground. The shock had however added neither to his knowledge nor imagination and he was again suspended in the air. This time he was allowed to hang so long that it was only after much labor that his blood was started in circulation.-- Frightened at their narrow escape from committing murder the settlers took a hasty departure, leaving the rope with Wiggy alike as a warning and a memento. The episode created a good deal of unfavorable comment at the time but it completely cured Wiggy of his tory proclivities.

Brant, when some time after he heard of a reflection made on his cruelty, by a resident of Cherry Valley, retorted that "he had never himself made war on women or children, nor," he added with emphasis "hanged a neighbor on suspicion."

John Foster was another resident whose Toryism was more pronounced than that of Wiggy Willson. Brant himself visited him the summer preceding the Massacre and there is little doubt but that he was in constant communication with the Indian and Tory leaders. It seems somewhat singular but apparently after the war all ill feeling between the patriots and the tories appears to have been dropped, so far at least as this settlement was concerned.-- Foster continued to live here many years after the close of war and was always well treated. In fact "Old Jacky Foster" became quite popular during his later years. Foster and Willson were both illiterate men.

During the following summer occurred the remarkable defence and escape of Robert Shankland, of which all the Border Histories of New York speak. Mr. Shankland, having taken his family to the Mohawk after the Massacre, returned the following summer with son, a boy of about 14 years, to harvest his crops. He was awakened one night by a pounding on the door of his log cabin. Getting up he found that the Indians were trying to chop through the door with their tomahawks. Taking his spear in his hand he suddenly opened the door and charged on the Indians. Surprised at the suddenness of the unexpected attack they retreated a few feet, followed by Mr. Shankland, who, in driving his spear at one of them, struck it in a log so hard that he broke the handle in trying to pull it out. Stooping down he grasped the blade, and wrenching it from the log, returned to the house without a shot being fired at him. Awakening his son he took his guns and began returning the fire which the Indians now commenced on the house, the boy loading as he fired. Despairing of accomplishing anything by this method of warfare, the Indians gathered a quantity of inflammable material, and placing it against the side of the cabin, fired it.-- During the excitement attendant upon this the boy attempted to escape from the house but was captured by the Indians. He was some time afterwards released. When he grew to manhood he moved to Cooperstown and became a person of considerable importance, having been a National Elector in 1808.

Mr. Shankland kept up his firing on the Indians, until the heat became too great for him to remain longer in the burning building, when he bethought himself of a cellar door close up to which grew a field of hemp. Creeping through this he was fortunate enough to escape through the hemp unperceived by the Indians, who continued dancing, yelling and shooting around the house until it was burned to the ground. Then they continued on their way, happy in the thought that the bones of the supposed victim were buried in the ashes of his dwelling.

The peace of the settlement was undisturbed during the following year and confidence was beginning to return to the settlers, when, without warning, on the 24th of April, 1780, a party of seventy-nine Indians and two tories descended on the ill-fated settlement. Eight of the settlers were killed and fourteen carried into captivity, and the settlement was this time completely wiped out of existence; the Fort, church and the few buildings left after the first incursion being burned to the ground. Thus in a few hours were the results of the labors and struggles of nearly forty years destroyed; the valley returned again into the undisputed possession of the beasts and the birds, and Cherry Valley, a few years before, the largest and most prominent of the Frontier settlements of New York, was but a name.

NAMES OF OTHER PRE-MASSACRE RESIDENTS
abstracted from
History of Cherry Valley

John Lindesay, a Scotch gentleman, settled in the valley in 1740. When he erected his modest house on the hill where now stands the residence of Edward Phelon, he was on the furthermost western bounds of civilization.

The following year a party of Scotch-Irish from Londonderry, New Hampshire, brought hither their scanty goods and settled. With them came the Rev. Samuel Dunlop, a graduate of Trinity College, Dublin. There were seven families in the original Londonderry party, comprising about thirty persons in all, including children. The names of the heads of five of these families,--David Ramsey, William Gault, James Campbell, Patrick Davidson and William Dickson,--have come down to us.

Mr. Lindesay, tired of the rough life and the severity of the winters, disposed of his farm in 1744 to a Mr. John Wells; a man of rare attainments and integrity, and possessed of a natural judicial mind. He was for many years judge and jury in all disputations that arose from time to time in the neighborhood, and after its formation was one of the Judges of Tryon County.

In the early fifties the little settlement received an impetus from the arrival of new settlers and from that time up to the beginning of the Revolution its growth, if slow, was steady and constant. Thus the records show that the eight families, who composed the population of the place in 1752, had increased to forty in 1765 and at the opening of the Revolution to over sixty.

The additions to the original settlers came mainly from the New England colonies, and, after the last French war, a number of French Canadians also took up their residence here. The former were mainly Scotch-Irish Presbyterians, who naturally passed by the Dutch settlements along the Mohawk and Schoharie Valleys to seek a section whose people held views more similar to their own, and where they could worship in a church of their own denomination.

At the meeting held to form the General Organization of the Tryon County Militia on 26 August 1775, among the officers appointed from Cherry Valley were: Samuel Clyde-Chairman & Adjutant & Captain, Robert Wells-First-Major, James Cannon, John Campbell Jr. and Robert Campbell, Lieutenants.

During the early days of the Revolution the families of Johnsons and Butlers, Tories, fled to Canada.

On the 5th of October, 1785, at a meeting of the "ancient inhabitants" the Presbyterian Society was re-organized and the meeting attended by the following, all named as inhabitants of Cherry Valley before the massacre: Col. Samuel Clyde, John Campbell Jr., James Willson, Robert Shankland, William Thompson, Samuel Ferguson, James Moore Jr., John Campbell Jr., Hugh Mitchell, William Gault, James Cannon, Samuel Campbell Jr., Samuel Clyde, Samuel Campbell, William Dickson, James Dickson, Daniel McCollum, John McKellip, Israel Wilson, James Wilson, Benjamin Dickson and John Dunlap. Two newcomers who attended the meeting were Thomas Whiticar and Luther Rich.

INDEX

A

Alden, Ichabod 11, 12, 13, 14, 30, 31
Allen, Ethan 24

B

Baptiste, Jean 23
Beardsley, Levi 4
Bearfoot, Isaac 28
Bierman, Richard 34
Blumenstock, Fred 34
Brant, Joseph 4, 10, 11, 12, 13, 18, 19, 28, 39
  Mary 32
  Molly 28
Bryant, William C. 29
Bush, Elijah 34
Butler, John 21, 22
  Walter 12, 19

C

Campbell, --- (Col.) 9, 10, 11, 12, 15, 21, 24, 25, 26, 35
--- (Mr.) 27
--- (Mrs.) 18, 19, 20, 21, 22, 23, 24, 25
Dewitt C. 34
Frank 34
James 6, 23, 24, 33, 34, 42
James S. 26
Jane 16
John 33, 43
Robert 26, 43
Samuel 8, 33, 36, 43
W. W. 3
Campbell, William 16, 34
  William W. 4, 26, 36
Cannon, --- (Capt.) 15
  --- (Mr.) 16
  Eleanor 19, 20
  James 37, 43
  Matthew 33
Claus, Daniel 28, 29
Clinton, --- (Gov.) 21, 24, 36
  DeWitt 3
  James 19
Clyde, --- (Col.) 12, 14, 15, 35
  --- (Maj.) 9
  Agnes 14, 15
  James D. 34
  Samuel 8, 36, 43
Coonrads, --- 34
Coons, --- 34
Cox, --- (Col.) 9
  A. B. (Mrs.) 33
Culley, --- 34

D

Davidson, Patrick 34, 42
Deserontyon, John 29
Dickson, --- 34
  Benjamin 43
  James 43
  William 6, 42, 43
Dunlap, John 43
Dunlop, Samuel 5, 6, 7, 11, 13, 15, 33, 35, 37, 42

E

Ellet, --- (Mrs.) 26

F

Ferguson, Samuel 43
Fiske, John 4
Flint, Elisha 33
Foster, John 34, 39
Frey, John 7, 37

G

Garrett, --- (Ensign) 30
Gault, --- 34
  William 6, 42
Germaine, George 9
Grant, --- (Gen.) 27

H

Haldimand, --- (Gov.) 32
Hammond, Jabez D. 4
Hand, --- (Gen.) 29
Hart, Roswell (Mrs.) 12
Head, George (Mrs.) 34
Herkimer, --- (Gen.) 9, 36
Hickling, --- (Capt.) 31
Hinckley, E. L. 34
Holden, --- (Lt.) 30
Horton, James 34

J

Jay, John 3
Johns, Catharine 28
Johnson, William 8, 28

K

Klock, --- (Col.) 10, 29

L

LaFayette, --- (Gen.) 10
Lindesay, --- (Mr.) 36
  John 5, 6, 7, 42
  Little Aaron 13

M

M'Kean, --- (Capt.) 34, 35, 36
M'Kown, --- 34
Marks, --- 34
McClellan, --- 34
McCollum, Daniel 43
McKellip, John 43
McKellips, --- 34
McKendry, William 11, 17
Millson, Jackson 33
Mitchell, Hugh 17, 19, 34, 37, 43
Montour, Catrine 16
Moore, --- (Mrs.) 20
  Elisha 34
  James 33, 43
  John 8, 9, 34, 35
  John (Mrs.) 18
Morse, James O. 4

N

Nelson, --- 33
Newberry, --- 17, 19
Niagara, Mary
  Deyonwadonti 29
Nott, Eliphalet 2, 3

P

Peck, William F. 28
Phelon, --- 34
  Edward 12, 42

R

Ramsay, David 6
Ramsey, David 42
Rich, Luther 43
Riches, James 11

S

Schuyler, --- (Gen.) 21
Scott, --- 34
Seelye, Isaac 4
Shankland, --- 34
  Robert 39, 40, 43
  Thomas 37
Sherman, C. W. 34
Sitz, Peter 10, 11
Spencer, Thomas 37
Stacy, --- (Col.) 30
  --- (Lt. Col.) 12, 13
Steenburgh, Chauncey 34
Stewart, Alvan 4
Sullivan, --- (Gen.) 23
Swinnerton, --- (Rev. Mr.) 36

T

Thompson, --- 34
  Alexander 38
  John 38
  William 43
Thornton, Matthew 14
Tryon, William 8
Turner, --- (Mrs.) 25, 26

W

Waldron, William H. 34
Warren, --- (Capt.) 17
  Benjamin 29
Washington, --- (Gen.) 24, 25, 27
Wells, --- 34
  --- (Mr.) 12, 13, 14
  Jane 21
  John 7, 13, 36, 37, 42
  Robert 13, 37, 43
White, Delos 4
  Joseph 4
  Menzo 4
Whiticar, Thomas 43
Whiting, --- (Maj.) 31
Wikoff, James 34
Williams, Eleazer 23
Willson, --- 34, 39
  James 34, 36, 43
  John 34, 36
  Louis G. 34
Wilson, --- 38
  Israel 43
  James 43
Wormuth, --- (Lt.) 38
  Matthew 10

www.ingramcontent.com/pod-product-compliance
Lightning Source LLC
Chambersburg PA
CBHW061515040426
42450CB00008B/1635